Kiss, Then Tell
Related One Act Plays

by Greg Cummings

Single copies of plays are sold for reading purposes only. The copying or duplicating of a play, or any part of play, by hand or by any other process, is an infringement of the copyright. Such infringement will be vigorously prosecuted.

Baker's Plays
7611 Sunset Blvd.
Los Angeles, CA 90042
bakersplays.com

NOTICE

This book is offered for sale at the price quoted only on the understanding that, if any additional copies of the whole or any part are necessary for its production, such additional copies will be purchased. The attention of all purchasers is directed to the following: this work is fully protected under the copyright laws of the United States of America, the British Commonwealth, including Canada, and all other countries of the Copyright Union. Violations of the Copyright Law are punishable by fine or imprisonment, or both. The copying or duplication of this work or any part of this work, by hand or by any process, is an infringement of the copyright and will be vigorously prosecuted.

This play may not be produced by amateurs or professionals for public or private performance without first submitting application for performing rights. Royalties are due on all performances whether for charity or gain, or whether admission is charged or not. Since performance of this play without the payment of the royalty fee renders anybody participating liable to severe penalties imposed by the law, anybody acting in this play should be sure, before doing so, that the royalty fee has been paid. Professional rights, reading rights, radio broadcasting, television and all mechanical rights, etc. are strictly reserved. Application for performing rights should be made directly to BAKER'S PLAYS.

No one shall commit or authorize any act or omission by which the copyright of, or the right to copyright, this play may be impaired. No one shall make any changes in this play for the purpose of production.

Publication of this play does not imply availability for performance. Both amateurs and professionals considering a production are strongly advised in their own interest to apply to Baker's Plays for written permission before starting rehearsals, advertising, or booking a theatre.

Whenever the play is produced, the author's name must be carried in all publicity, advertising and programs. Also, the following notice must appear on all printed programs, "Produced by special arrangement with Baker's Plays."

Licensing fees for KISS, THEN TELL is based on a per performance rate and payable one week in advance of the production.

Please consult the Baker's Plays website at www.bakersplays.com or our current print catalogue for up to date licensing fee information.

Copyright © 2009 by Greg Cummings
Made in U.S.A.
All rights reserved.

KISS, THEN TELL
ISBN **978-0-87440-231-5**
1883-B

KISS, THEN TELL was first produced at the Jolla Country Day School in La Jolla, California on Friday, February 5, 1999. The production was directed by Greg Cummings. The cast was as follows:

GARY	Sam Hodgson
ELISE	Elise Kerr
TEDDY	Jacob Gelfand
SOOKI	Lindsey Reed
VALERIE	Amy Sanderson
STACK	Josh White
COACH	Scott Sanderson
JEFF	Kenner Michael
KELLY	Wendy Smith
ALICE	Jessica Spaulding
SAMUEL	Michael Salk
BETTY	Jessica Johnson
BILLY	Jacob Gelfand
ROSIE	Amy Sanderson
RICHARD	David Birnbaum
WAYNE	Michael Blumberg
CHELSEA	Amy Sanderson

For Gisela Fritzsching,
mentor and friend

TABLE OF CONTENTS

Love Bites 7

My Li'l DiCaprio 13

Brace Yourself. 19

Two Good Pilgrims 25

Mysterious Ways 31

After Math 37

The Beauty and the Beast Within. 43

Forewarned is Forearmed 49

Arcane Traditions 57

LOVE BITES

CHARACTERS

JENNIFER - Ten.

GARY - Nine.

SCENE

The school cafeteria.

TIME

Noon.

PROPS

Sandwich,
Pudding cup,
Spoon.

COSTUMES

Everyday school clothes for both.

(AT RISE: JENNIFER, ten, and GARY, nine, eat their respective lunches.)

(GARY has just taken a bite of her sandwich and is in the process of handing it back to her. According to GARY, this was their "first kiss.")

GARY. Wow! Wow!

JENNIFER. Wow?

GARY. Man oh man!

JENNIFER. *(looks around to see if they're being observed)* Gary! Shh.

GARY. Thanks for the "sandwich", Jennifer!

JENNIFER. You're welcome, Gary.

(looking around) Shh.

GARY. Lettuce! Bologna! And Strawberry Preserves! What a "sandwich"!

JENNIFER. My mommy's kinda quirky.

GARY. Quirky? I don't think so! Deee-licious, maybe!

JENNIFER. *(smiles)* Maybe.

(eating her sandwich)

Must be tough.

GARY. Tough?

JENNIFER. Being the new kid in town.

(GARY stifles a giggle.)

JENNIFER. And forgetting your lunch.

(GARY stifles a giggle.)

JENNIFER. For the third day in a row.

(GARY stifles a giggle.)

GARY. *(stops giggling)* Sorry.

(doubles over, stifling his giggles)

JENNIFER. Gary? Are you O.K.? Would you like me to call Mrs. Nedrow?

GARY. *(giggling)* I...just...never...kissed...a...girl...before!

JENNIFER. Kissed a girl...?

GARY. Oh, I mean I had a girlfriend before, at my old school, of course.

JENNIFER. Gary?

GARY. Did I say girlfriend? Girlfriend*s*! Plural on that: Girlfriends!

JENNIFER. Gary?!

GARY. *(coyly)* Like you couldn't tell.

(sidles next to her on the bench)

JENNIFER. *(standing)* GARY!

GARY. What?

JENNIFER. Gary!

(looking around) We didn't kiss!

GARY. I bit your sandwich.

JENNIFER. That's not kissing!

GARY. Oh, it is where I come from!

JENNIFER. Here we call it lunch!

GARY. You let me have a bite of your sandwich!

JENNIFER. You haven't eaten lunch in three days, Gary! Mrs. Nedrow was getting worried about you.

GARY. I bit right next to the spot where you bit!

JENNIFER. Mrs. Nedrow *told* me to, Gary!

(pause) She told me to...share.

(turns to go)

Lunch is almost over, anyway...

GARY. I'm sorry.

(takes from his pocket a pudding dessert cup)

JENNIFER. *(turning to face him)* Gary? Is that…?

GARY. *(sadly)* Pudding. Choco-Vanilla Swirl. They take chocolate and vanilla and they swirl 'em together. My mom usually forgets to make me a sandwich so I just find something in the refrigerator.

(JENNIFER returns and sits next to GARY on the bench.)

JENNIFER. *(entranced)* Choco-Vanilla Swirl Pudding!

GARY. Is it your favorite?

JENNIFER. *(nodding)* My mom never lets me have sweets. Ever.

GARY. *(taking a spoon from his other pocket)* I…only have one spoon.

(He scoops some pudding onto his spoon. He brings the spoon to his mouth.)

GARY. I'm sorry. Would you like to…?

(offers the spoon to her)

JENNIFER. *(smiles)* That's OK, Gary. You start…

(GARY eats the first spoonful. He offers the next to her.)

(They close their eyes and smile. It's as if they're about to kiss.)

(fade to black)

The End

MY LI'L DICAPRIO

CHARACTERS

BRADLEY - Ten.
AMY - Ten.

SCENE

The school bus stop.

TIME

Morning.

COSTUMES

Everyday school clothes for both.

(SETTING: *A school bus stop.*)

(AT RISE: BRADLEY *and* AMY *are seated. They've just kissed.*)

(*They open their eyes.*)

BRADLEY. *(ecstatic)* Oh! Amy! I'm...speechless!

AMY. *(faking speechlessness)* Oh! I'm...me, too!

(*trying to remember*)

Bradley....

BRADLEY. *(closing his eyes)* The delight of that kiss! Amy! Ecstasy! Oh!

AMY. *(closes her eyes but peeks, trying hard to feel his ecstasy)* And...oh: your lips!

(*remembering*)

Bradley!

BRADLEY. *(eyes closed)* Lips like sweet, mushy, summer rain clouds ready to burst!

AMY. *(peeking)* Yes. Yes. Your lips...were...mushy! Mush, too, yes! Bradley!

BRADLEY. Minty clouds!

AMY. *(faking it)* Minty! Yes, Minty!

BRADLEY. Like a minty rain forest! A peppermint jungle growth!

AMY. This morning I used Crest Mint Ultra With Sparkles!

BRADLEY. I remember now! Our lips together made that sound, that little sound baby robins make when they take food from their mothers! Pecking! Pecking! Ah!

AMY. Yes!

(*trying hard to keep up*)

The touch...and the...taste...and...the sounds...of nature. Of...love!?

BRADLEY. *(sniffing)* I'm smelling a meadow! And remembering our kiss!

AMY. *(sniffing)* I'm smelling....

BRADLEY. Awash! Aglow! With my memories! Our kiss! Oh, our kiss! My senses are alive, Amy!

AMY. *(finally getting it)* Mine, too, Bradley!

BRADLEY. Really? Really, Amy?

AMY. Oh, Bradley, when we kissed! Your eyelids...

BRADLEY. My eyelids?

AMY. Your eyelids fluttered! They were butterflies!

BRADLEY. *(opening his eyes)* Excuse me?

AMY. *(keeping her eyes closed)* Monarch butterflies! Dancing!

BRADLEY. *(upset)* You're not supposed to kiss with your eyes open, Amy!

AMY. *(oblivious)* Your eyeballs were rolling! Like you were sleeping! Like when we dream! Like my Li'l DiCaprio!

BRADLEY. *(angrily)* Like your Li'l DiCaprio? Like your dog?! I kiss like your dog?!

(**AMY** *opens her eyes.*)

AMY. *(suddenly sad)* He's not my Li'l DiCaprio any more, Bradley. I gave him to my little brother. I have to live with just my mom, now. My brother lives with just my dad. And they have to live two hours away now. So I told my brother that Li'l DiCaprio could be like his Saint Bernard dog. Like when I couldn't be there for him, he could still be rescued by a big mountain dog that could save him. My little brother's only three. *(pause)* I'm not there with him anymore. *(cries)* Like when he...needs to be rescued.

(**AMY** *closes her eyes.*)

BRADLEY. *(also sad now)* Amy...

(pause, then barks like a dog)

Woof!

(no response)

Woof!

AMY. *(eyes still closed)* Bradley?

*(**BRADLEY** sits on the ground next to her.)*

BRADLEY. Woof!

AMY. *(starting to smile)* Bradley?

BRADLEY. Woof! Woof!

AMY. *(smiling)* Bradley, are you rescuing…me?

BRADLEY. *(laughing)* Woof, woof, woof!

AMY. *(smiling broadly)* Oh, Bradley!

(pets the top of his head and scratches the back of his neck, as if he were her dog)

AMY. *(suddenly sad again)* My Li'l Di Caprio.

(still petting his head)

(fade to black)

The End

BRACE YOURSELF

KISS, THEN TELL

CHARACTERS

TEDDY - Twelve.
SOOKI - Twelve.

SCENE

School lunch bench.

TIME

Noon.

PROPS

Two school lunch bags.

COSTUMES

Everyday school clothes for both.

TEDDY. *(in darkness)* Ow!

(AT RISE: TEDDY *and* SOOKI, *both twelve, sitting on the bench. They've just kissed. Their school lunch bags are next to them.)*

TEDDY. *(to* SOOKI, *holding his mouth)* Ow!

SOOKI. Oh, Teddy! I'm sorry!

TEDDY. *(garbled)* Sooki! You should've told me!

SOOKI. What? I'm sorry. I can't understand you.

TEDDY. You should've told me that you wear braces!

SOOKI. *(sincerely)* I'm sorry, Teddy. I should've told you.

TEDDY. *(garbled)* Before we kissed!

SOOKI. I just got them the other day I was too embarrassed they make me look so…

TEDDY. I'm bleeding!

SOOKI. Let me see. You're not bleeding.

TEDDY. *(garbled)* I bet I am!

SOOKI. You *used to* wear braces, Teddy!

TEDDY. *(garbled)* We didn't start kissing until *last week*, Sooki! I got my braces off in August! I protected you! I saved you from MY braces! I…

SOOKI. I have a cold! I have a stuffy nose!

TEDDY. *(garbled, mocking her)* "I had to open my mouth! To kiss you, Teddy! Teddy dear"!

SOOKI. Teddy! I had to BREATHE!

TEDDY. *(mocking)* Oooh: breathing!

SOOKI. I was losing oxygen!

TEDDY. First, you open your mouth to kiss me! Disgusting enough!

SOOKI. I was blacking out!

TEDDY. And then I discover your braces! On my lips!

SOOKI. Teddy! Can we please just do our science homework?

(takes a jar from her school lunch bag)

I brought the chameleons...

TEDDY. First I treat your lips like a palace, and then you treat mine like a rusty fence!

(hallucinating)

I need to get a shot! A tetanus shot! Too late! I have lockjaw!

(through a clenched jaw)

What are you doing, Sooki? What is that?

(She pulls a small tin from her lunch bag.)

SOOKI. Tiger balm.

TEDDY. Tiger balm?

SOOKI. I stole it. From Cynthia. Sh.

TEDDY. You stole this?

(pause)

Who's Cynthia?

SOOKI. My dad's new wife.

TEDDY. Your dad got married? Again?

SOOKI. Number four.

TEDDY. *(stunned)* Who was number three?

(pause)

SOOKI. I forget.

(pause)

Cynthia's O.K., I guess. She thinks she's "New Age."

TEDDY. New Age?

SOOKI. She feng shui-ed my room.

TEDDY. *(pretending he understands)* Sorry.

SOOKI. It's not so bad.

> *(re: the Tiger Balm)*
>
> She knows I steal her stuff; she says it's all part of my "adjustment period."
>
> *(pause)* Hold still.

TEDDY. What are you doing?

SOOKI. *(reading the Tiger Balm tin)* "The soothing properties of Tiger Balm must be applied topically, to maximize its ancient healing medicine."

> *(pause)*
>
> Give me your lips, Teddy.
>
> *(no response)*
>
> Teddy?

TEDDY. *(sullenly turning away)* I don't know, Sooki. There are so many changes going on. Sixth grade. New academic pressures. Your braces. Cynthia. Our relationship seems to be…

SOOKI. Teddy: I'm your girlfriend. You're my boyfriend. Now close your eyes.

> *(He does.)*
>
> Now stick out your lips.
>
> *(He doesn't.)*
>
> Cynthia told my father that everything in his life can now be healed. She uses Tiger Balm all the time.
>
> She uses it all over the house. My cat stopped shedding. I don't know.
>
> *(**TEDDY** opens his eyes.)*
>
> *(with sadness, looking away from **TEDDY**)*
>
> My dad looks happy, happier than I've seen him in a

long time.

(sadly)

I just don't know anymore…

*(**TEDDY** closes his eyes and puckers his lips.)*

SOOKI. Thanks, Teddy.

(re: his lips)

Hm. They are a little raw, aren't they? Sorry about that.

(applies some balm to his lips)

Cynthia says that relationships need to experience constant change, Teddy. They need to change to survive.

(not understanding what she's just said)

You're a good boyfriend, Teddy.

(continues to apply the balm to his lips)

(fade to black)

The End

TWO GOOD PILGIRMS

KISS, THEN TELL

CHARACTERS

VALERIE - Sixteen. Cheerleader.
JOHN - Sixteen. Football Player.
COACH - Adult.

SCENE

A bench on the sidelines of the football field.

TIME

Football practice.

PROPS

A copy of the play, *Romeo and Juliet.*

COSTUMES

Cheerleader uniform for the girl;
Football practice clothes for the boy.

(*SETTING: A bench on the sidelines of the football field.*)

(*AT RISE:* **VALERIE** *and* **JOHN** *sit on the bench. She wears her cheerleading outfit. He is all suited up for football practice.*)

(*Their eyes are closed. They've just kissed. He quickly opens his eyes. Her eyes remain closed;* **STACK** *doesn't notice.*)

STACK. (*pumping his arm in victory*) Yes! Touchdown!

(*smacking his lips*)

Great kiss, Valerie! Great kiss! Number one: your personal best! Number two: "Extra point! It's good!"

(*realizes*)

Sorry. My bad: I'm a pig.

(*hitting himself*)

I'm a pig I'm a pig! I'm a pig!

(*starting to realize*)

Wait a minute. Question: Valerie? I've *always* been a pig, but you never said anything. I went to football camp this summer. You went to cheerleading camp AND THEN you did a new thing. You went to that... drama camp? Drama Camp. Did you...?

VAL. (*eyes still closed*) "Good pilgrim..."

STACK. Good pilgrim?

COACH. (*from off left*) Stackniweicz?! Stackniweicz!

STACK. (*standing rigidly*) Coach.

(*gulps in fear*)

COACH. Get your butt over here, Stack!

STACK. *(to off left)* Coach! Over here, Coach! I'm here, Coach! Coming, coach!

(to VAL)

It's Coach. I gotta go.

(turns to go, turns back to her)

My bad: Question: am I being a pig again? You gotta tell me. Brainstorm: Want another kiss?

COACH. *(from off left)* Stackniweicz!

STACK. *(winking at VAL)* You know… "one for the road"?

VAL. *(eyes still closed)* "Good pilgrim, you do wrong your hand too much.

Which mannerly devotion shows in this."

STACK. *(gulps in fear)* "…mannerly devotion…"?

VAL. "For saints have hands that pilgrims' hands do touch,

And palm to palm is holy palmers' kiss."

STACK. A light bulb in Stack's brain! Stack gets it: Drama Camp! That Drama Camp you went to this summer! That's where you're getting all this!

(pumps his arm)

Touchdown!

COACH. *(from off left)* Move it, Stackniweicz! Move it or lose it!

STACK. *(to off left)* Be right there, Coach!

(to VAL)

That's Coach. I gotta move it or lose it.

(picks up his helmet)

Drama Camp. Weird. So… "one for the road"?

(winks at her)

VAL. *(standing)* "Ay, pilgrim, lips that they must use in prayer."

(She opens her eyes and turns to face him.)

(STACK reels.)

VAL. "Saints do not move, though grant for prayer's sake."

(closes her eyes and prepares herself for STACK's kiss)

COACH. *(from off left)* That's it, Stackniweicz, that's it! Laps! Ten laps! Now!

STACK. *(reeling between the two choices)* Laps? Or lips? Lips? Or laps? Which one of these? Which one of these?

(closes his eyes, leans to kiss VAL)

COACH. *(from off left)* Oh my God! Don't do it! Don't do it, Stack!

(VAL opens her eyes, spins, and crosses stage right.)

COACH. *(from off left)* No! Tomorrow's our season opener!

(STACK falls to the ground.)

COACH. *(from off left)* Think of your energy level, boy! Think of your electrolytes!

(STACK, groggy, sits on the bench. He finds a book which VAL left for him.)

STACK/VAL. *(he reading/she reciting the book's title)* "Romeo and Juliet"

COACH. *(from off left, despairing at the potential loss of his star player)* Shakespeare?!

(weeping)

Squat Thrusts, boy! You'll do Squat Thrusts!

STACK. Romeo and Juliet?

(She crosses to him and sits next to him on the bench.)

VAL. My Romeo.

COACH. *(despairing) (from off left)* Defense, boy!

STACK. *(dazed, to* **VAL***)* Juliet?

COACH. *(from off left)* Defense!

   (weeps)

VAL. *(smiling sweetly in victory)* "You kiss by the book."

COACH. *(from off left, grasping at straws)* Get outta there, boy! Leave the pocket! Scramble!

Leave the field if you have to! We've practiced this, for God's sake! Find daylight! Head for the daylight! Visualize! See yourself in the end zone and there you are! There you are!

STACK. *(reading a marked passage from the play)* "Sin from my lips? O trespass sweetly urged. Give me my sin again."

COACH. *(from off left, hallucinating)* Wriggle, boy! Wriggle free! Dig! Dig in!

VAL/STACK. *(she reciting, he reading another marked passage)* "Two households, both alike in dignity, in fair Verona where we lay our scene..."

COACH. *(from off left, screaming)* For God's sake, boy: Punt!

   *(***VAL** *and* **STACK** *close their eyes and lean in to kiss.)*

   (From off left, the **COACH** *sobs.)*

   (fade to black)

The End

MYSTERIOUS WAYS

CHARACTERS

JEFF - middle schooler.
KELLY - middle schooler.

SCENE

Bench in the garden of a parochial school.

TIME

The school day has just ended.

PROPS

A cell phone, car horn (off stage).

COSTUMES

Parochial school uniforms for both.

(SETTING: A park bench.)

(AT RISE: In darkness, church bells chime.)

JEFF/KELLY. *(in darkness)* Oh! My! God! No! Nooo!

(Lights reveal JEFF *and* KELLY, *each dressed in their Catholic school uniforms. They kneel at each end of the bench, and pray. They've just kissed.)*

JEFF/KELLY. *(to each other and God, variously)* Oh my God! Kissing? You!? Me kissing you!? Out here? In the open? In the daylight hours? There's the church! Oh, the church chimes! The church chimes of doom! Who do you think you are? Who do I think I am? Who do you think YOU are? Where do you think we are? Sodom? Gomorrah? Oh my God!

(looking heavenward)

Heaven. HE saw us kiss.

(bow their heads in shame)

KELLY. Now we're just animals, Jeff. We're no better than...

JEFF. There were animals in The Garden, Kelly.

KELLY. You're rationalizing again, Jeff.

JEFF. *(looking up at a tree, offstage)* Sh.

KELLY. You're right again, Jeff. Silent penance can be our only penance, now.

*(*KELLY *bows her head and prays.)*

JEFF. No. Kelly. Look.

(pointing to the tree)

KELLY. *(looking)* Squirrel?

JEFF. *(correcting her)* Chipmunk.

KELLY. Chipmunk?

JEFF. Look at his tail.

KELLY. Look at him. He's cute. Look at him run and jump.

JEFF. Look.

KELLY. Now he's eating.

JEFF. There are two of them.

KELLY. *(smiling)* Two chipmunks! Running. Jumping. Eating.

JEFF. *(assuredly)* God's creatures.

KELLY. Playing.

> *(pause)*
>
> Playing together.
>
> *(to JEFF)*
>
> What are you looking at? What are you looking for?

JEFF. *(looking in the sky and joking)* Thunderbolts.

KELLY. *(not understanding)* Thunderbolts?

JEFF. Thunderbolts. Lightning. Floods. Forty days and forty nights.

> *(smiling)* "Animals" kissing in "The Garden," after all.

KELLY. *(finally smiling)* Locusts.

JEFF. *(smiling)* Locusts?

KELLY. *(smiling)* Locusts.

JEFF/KELLY. *(joking)* No! Plague! The Plague! The Black Death! The earth is rent! He razes our village to the ground! We are swallowed up! No longer in His favor! The darkness! Our ingratitude! He gave us so much and now.. Chipmunks! Chipmunks! Run! Hide! Save yourselves! Don't store up for the winter! There is no time! No time! No…

> *(They roll on the ground, laughing.)*
>
> *(They stop laughing and look at each other on the ground. They lean in to kiss.)*
>
> *(From Offstage Left, a car horn.)*

KELLY. *(standing, suddenly terrified)* My father!

> *(to JEFF)*
>
> Hide, dammit!
>
> *(to offstage, sweetly)*
>
> Coming, Daddy!
>
> *(to JEFF, as if he were Satan)*
>
> At school tomorrow? Don't talk to me!
>
> *(starts to leave, turns back)*
>
> Don't EVER talk to me! EVER!
>
> *(faces offstage and pastes a smile on her face)*
>
> Daddy?! Where have you been? I've been waiting all afternoon for you!
>
> *(exits)*
>
> *(pause)*
>
> *(The sky darkens.)*

JEFF. Damn.

> *(distant thunder)*

JEFF. Damn.

> *(taking a cell phone from his pocket, punching a number, listening)*
>
> Mommy? Mommy, can you pick me up? I'm at St. Mary's. Soon? Thanks, Mommy. It's starting to rain. Mommy? Nothing.
>
> *(pause)*
>
> I'm sorry.
>
> *(fade to black)*

The End

AFTER MATH

CHARACTERS

SAMUEL - Fifteen.
ALICE - Fifteen.

SCENE

A high school math lab.

TIME

Between classes.

PROPS

Two of each:
Pocket protectors,
Calculators,
Graphs,
Protractors.

COSTUMES

Each wears a lab coat and glasses.

(SETTING: *A high school math classroom.*)

(AT RISE: SAMUEL *and* ALICE, *feverishly work their pocket calculators. They both wear wrinkled clothing, glasses, and pocket protectors. They sit amidst a pile of charts, graphs, protractors, and computers. They've just kissed.*)

ALICE. *(not looking up from her work)* Samuel?

(no response)

Samuel?

SAMUEL. *(not looking up from his work)* Oh, Alice! Not to worry! Our NEXT kiss will be even MORE precise! Even more delineated! Even more...

ALICE. *(not looking up from her work)* But, Samuel? We'd been planning that first kiss since last semester. It took us fifteen weeks of laboratory testing before we even tried to...

SAMUEL. *(not looking up from his work)* Vector!

ALICE. Vector?

SAMUEL. *(not looking up from his work)* The problem was in the trajectory of our opposing vectors!

ALICE. Opposing...?

SAMUEL. And...acute! Eee!

ALICE. *(not hearing correctly, blushing)* "I'm cute? I'm a cutie?" Oh, Samuel...

SAMUEL. *(not noticing, not looking up from his work)* Acute angles? Acute angles? Eee. What were we thinking? Acute angles were uncalled for! Completely uncalled for! Obtuse angles! That's the ticket!

ALICE. *(rejected)* Oh. Not "a cute." Acute. Obtuse.

SAMUEL. *(not looking up from his work)* No wonder our chins were thrown all out of whack! Our trajectories were off!

ALICE. *(dejected)* Our trajectories. Are out of whack.

SAMUEL. *(not looking up from his work)* As was our drag

coefficient! No wonder our initial lip impact was off by...eight point four degrees! Eee!

ALICE. *(re:* SAMUEL*)* Obtuse. Out of whack. Drag coefficient. Drag...

(turns left, starts to exit)

SAMUEL. *(not noticing, not looking up from his work)* And...yes!... increasing the "leaning in" quotient of our bodies, we should form...one perfect isosceles triangle!

(stands to go)

ALICE. *(stops)* Samuel, where are you going?

SAMUEL. To get some string! An incline! A pulley! And maybe...a socket wrench!

(starts to exit right)

ALICE. *(summoning courage)* Samuel!

SAMUEL. *(stunned, noticing her for the first time)* Alice?

(She tosses to the floor her protractor, her calculator, and her pocket protector.)

SAMUEL. *(stunned)* Alice. Your protractor. Your calculator. Your protector. Your protector...

(She tosses her glasses to the floor.)

SAMUEL. Alice! Your glasses!

ALICE. *(closing her eyes)* Oh, Samuel!

(stretches her arms like wings)

SAMUEL. *(inspired by her)* Oh, Alice!

(He closes his eyes, throws to the floor his protractor, his calculator, his protector and finally his glasses!)

(He stretches his arms like wings.)

ALICE. Oh, Samuel!

(opens her eyes)

SAMUEL. Oh, Alice!

> *(opens his eyes)*
>
> *(Having forsaken their charts and formulas, they turn to face each other.)*
>
> *(Unfortunately, They have also forsaken their glasses. Result: their love is nearly blind. They grope the air.)*

ALICE. Oh!

> *(pause)*
>
> Samuel?

SAMUEL. *(suddenly terrified)* My glasses!

> *(drops to the floor and feels about for his glasses)*

ALICE. *(emboldened)* Samuel?! Samuel?!

SAMUEL. I...can't...see.

> *(feels the floor for his glasses)*

ALICE. *(emboldened, resourceful)* Love...can be...blind, Samuel!

> *(hopeful)* Love IS blind.
>
> *(trying to appeal to his intellectual side)*
>
> I read that somewhere. In a book. In the library. On line.
>
> *(motionless, hopeful)*

SAMUEL. Love?

> *(long pause)*
>
> Love?
>
> *(slowly standing, realizing)*
>
> Why, yes. Yes, it is, Alice. Love is blind. I see that now.
>
> *(motionless)*

And yes, you're right, countless works of literature have been based on exactly that premise, presently proven by our own experience! *(motionless, still questioning)*

ALICE. *(finally getting an idea, she chants, somewhat timidly at first)* Ahhhhh.

SAMUEL. What are you doing, Alice?

ALICE. *(chanting)* Ahhhh.

(pause)

Love…can be blind, Samuel, but…

SAMUEL. *(finishing her sentence)* …but it can't be completely senseless!

ALICE. Yes! Yes! Oh!

(chanting)

Ahhhh!

SAMUEL. Alice! That sound! Your sound waves! Those nodes!

ALICE. *(coyly)* So…you think you know my nodes, do you?

(chanting)

Ahhhh!

SAMUEL. Oh, baby, I'd know your frequency anywhere!

(ALICE chants.)

(SAMUEL gropes his way to her.)

(fade to black)

The End

THE BEAUTY AND THE BEAST WITHIN

CHARACTERS

BILLY - Fourteen.
BETTY - Eighteen.

SCENE

The Macy's Cosmetics Counter.

TIME

Saturday afternoon.

PROPS

Hand mirror,
Bottle of Old Spice,
Cigarettes.

COSTUMES

Regular school clothes for Billy;
Cosmetics counter smock for Betty.

(*SETTING: Macy's Cosmetics Counter.*)

(*AT RISE:* **BILLY**, *fourteen and* **BETTY**, *eighteen, stand at the counter.* **BETTY** *wears her Macy's cosmetics counter smock.* **BILLY** *has just given her a surprise kiss. In response, she has just hit him.*)

BILLY. *(holding his nose)* Oh! I'm sorry I'm sorry I'm sorry!
BETTY. *(livid)* What the hell did you just do to me, squirt?!
BILLY. I said I'm sorry.

(*nearly overcome by the cosmetic counter smells*)

BETTY. *(looking in her compact mirror)* You smudged my makeup! Damn you, kid! You smudged me!
BILLY. *(delirious)* Don't tell anybody? Please?
BETTY. Don't tell anybody?! Don't tell anybody!? Kid, this is the Cosmetics Counter at Macy's! This is the center of the universe! The entire world saw what you did! You kissed me, you little freak!

(*noticing her boss, offstage*)

What? No! What? Oh, no. No.

(*forces a laugh*)

Of course not, Mrs. Thrombit! This little boy was just… he's buying…some lipstick…for his mommy!

(*to* **BILLY**)

Isn't that right, little boy? I said, Isn't that right, little boy?
BILLY. *(delirious)* I am so sorry.
BETTY. *(watching her boss exit)* Everything's fine, Mrs. Thrombit. Everything's under control. Everything's all under control.

(*to* **BILLY**)

Freeze, punk! Don't move a muscle! You...ninth grader from hell!

BILLY. *(woozy)* Eighth grader.

BETTY. What?

BILLY. *(reeling)* I'm in the eighth grade. I'm an...eighth grader from hell.

BETTY. Eighth grade?! I'm eighteen years old! I go to junior college! My boyfriend...my fiancé...is going to be a Navy Seal! Eighth grader?! He'll kill you!

BILLY. *(holding his stomach)* I'm sick.

BETTY. You are sick, kid! I took Intro to Psych. last semester. You are deranged!

BILLY. *(sitting down)* I'm gonna throw up.

BETTY. Not behind MY counter you're not!

(pushing him away)

BILLY. *(lying on the floor)* The fumes. The fumes...

BETTY. Fumes? Fumes? That's PAR-foom, kid! Parfum!

BILLY. *(gasping for air)* Parfum! Lipstick! Blush! Rouge! So many bottles, so many jars, so many sprays...

BETTY. I just pressed for security. They're calling your mommy.

BILLY. *(seeing visions)* Mommy?

(calling) Mommy?

BETTY. What a baby!

BILLY. *(hallucinating)* Do we have to go to Macy's today, Mommy? Why do we always have to go past the cosmetics counter, Mommy? Why don't we enter the mall by the hardware store?

BETTY. Turd.

BILLY. *(with new-found strength)* What?

BETTY. *(taken aback by his sudden forcefulness)* Excuse me?

BILLY. What did you just call me? You just called me a turd. *(no response)* You just called me a turd. Admit it. You called me a turd. Why?

(mocking)

"Because turds smell bad, Billy. Turds smell bad. You smell bad. Therefore, Billy, you smell like a turd!"

BILLY. *(cont.)* What's that, Betty? What's that? Some of your junior college logic? Well, I guess we have a little problem here, Betty! Because junior college logic doesn't work on Little Billy! Remember: Little Billy's just a little eighth grader from hell.

BETTY. What the hell is wrong with you, kid?

BILLY. Oh, let's see.

(sniffing)

Let's just call 'em pheromones, Betty.

BETTY. *(tense)* Pheromones?

BILLY. You have no idea what you do for a living, do you, Betty? Pheromones are powerful things. Powerful things. Excites the memories? Excites the glands? Excites the glands? You know what I'm talking 'bout, Betty. You excited, Betty? Your glands excited, are they? *(no response)* Nervous about losing your job? Your junior college work study? That barking seal "fiancé" of yours, Betty? Don't be.

(pats the floor next to him)

Come on down, girl.

(grabs a bottle from the counter, opens it, douses himself with it)

BETTY. *(inhaling, falling under his spell)* What…are you doing?

BILLY. *(proudly holds the bottle aloft)* Old Spice.

BETTY. *(inhaling, falling more deeply under his spell)* Old Spice.

(falls to the floor next to him)

(BILLY, acting as if he's twenty-six, takes a cigarette from her smock.)

BILLY. Old Spice, Betty. *Old* Spice.

(pause)

Mind if I smoke?

(no response) Got a light?

BETTY. Got a light? Oh my God!

(completely under his spell)

Come here, sailor!

(She grabs him by his collar, and pulls him close to her. She is about to kiss him.)

BILLY. *(quickly recovering, looks around and calls)* Mommy?

(fade to black)

The End

FOREWARNED IS FOREARMED

CHARACTERS

ROSIE - Thirteen.
RICHARD - Eighteen. Her brother.

SCENE

Rosie's room.
Sports star posters, suggestion of a bed.

TIME

Afternoon.

PROPS

Sports equipment,
Suitcase,
Two pillows.

COSTUMES

Athletic workout clothes for Rosie;
Traveling clothes for Richard.

(SETTING: The bedroom of Rosie, age 13. Posters of sports stars adorn every wall. About the room-every known piece of sporting equipment.)

(AT RISE: ROSIE sitting cross legged on the floor. Her eyes are closed. She wears athletic wear. She's kissing her forearm, to practice kissing a boy.)

ROSIE. Kenny. Kenny.

(stops kissing her arm, opens her eyes, then sarcastically)

Oh, yeah, I'm impressive. I'm hot. This'll work.

(She tries again. She closes her eyes. Again, she kisses her forearm.)

(RICHARD, her brother, holding his suitcase, rushes by her door.)

RICHARD. *(stopping briefly)* Hey! Rosie! Rosalinda! Hey! What're you doing?

ROSIE. *(caught, she quickly crosses her arms)* This is my room! Get out!

RICHARD. Sorry.

(re: his suitcase)

My train leaves in an hour.

ROSIE. Your train?!

RICHARD. Dad called. Something came up at work. I had to call a cab.

(checks his watch)

ROSIE. But...we were going to drive up! And we were going to leave tomorrow!

RICHARD. Dad just found out he's going to be busy all weekend. He needs the car.

ROSIE. But we were all going to drive you up to college all together! Mom...

RICHARD. Mom's still in Pennsylvania, you know that, taking care of grandma.

ROSIE. Oh, great! Just great!

RICHARD. I'll take the train today, and Dad says you can all come up next weekend. And you can bring me all the rest of my stuff.

ROSIE. No! Bring your own stuff!

RICHARD. Hey! Listen! You can get into all my gear and stuff all week and I'll never know!

ROSIE. Me? Get into your stuff?!

RICHARD. Oh! Like you're never into my stuff when I'm not home!

ROSIE. The only reason I would ever step foot into your room would be to torch it!

RICHARD. Fine!

(turns to go)

ROSIE. Just wait!

RICHARD. Football practice starts two weeks before classes! You know that!

ROSIE. But next weekend we can all go up together!

RICHARD. Rosie...

ROSIE. Fine! Fine!

RICHARD. Oh, that's attractive.

(looking out her window)

That's my cab.

ROSIE. So go!

(turns away from him)

RICHARD. *(turning to go)* I'll have enough trouble just making the team...

ROSIE. Great, Richard! Just great! The ONE THING we were going to do as a family! THE LAST THING we were going to do as a family! The last and most final thing we were ever going to get to do, as an activity, as an outing, as an adventure, something that could remind us of the family vacations we never took as a family because by the time I came around you were already on the starting team of every sport known to man, and we never got to go anywhere because every summer you had basketball camp or football camp or camp retardo or something and "Oh, there goes Ricky, boy, Rosie, your big brother sure can run!" Or pass! Or hit! Or kick! "Boy isn't that Ricky just.." He's just...

(overcome, she tries to hide her crying)

(RICHARD, *stunned, has stopped in her doorway.)*

RICHARD. *(trying to joke her out of it)* Rosie. Rosie. Hey. That was pretty good, Rosalinda. Maybe you should do Drama Club this year instead of field hockey.

(crosses to her)

ROSIE. Get out. You have to catch your cab.

(RICHARD *crosses to her window)*

RICHARD. *(yelling to the cab driver)* Cab? I'm sorry. I'm not ready yet! I...don't know when I'll be ready! I'm sorry! I'm sorry, sir!

(watches cab drive away)

Well, he's mad.

(no response)

This town's full of cabs. He'll never remember me.

(crosses back to her bed)

I'll just call Dad. Maybe I'll catch a later train.

(pause)

Listen, Rosie: you're gonna make the cut for field hockey.

ROSIE. *(sarcastically)* Yeah, right: *two* star athletes in the same family!

RICHARD. No. I...saw you practice yesterday.

ROSIE. *(wiping away her tears)* You came to my practice?

RICHARD. Well...I won't be seeing you for a while, and

(pause)

I heard your coaches talking and...

ROSIE. *(starting to smile)* You told Dad you went "college shopping" at the mall.

RICHARD. They said you were great. Your coaches said they needed you on first string.

(sits on her bed next to her)

So.

ROSIE. So.

RICHARD. So...*(attempting coy)* So, you like that new boy?

ROSIE. What?

RICHARD. That new kid, Kenny. He's in your grade?

ROSIE. Yeah.

RICHARD. So?

ROSIE. So?

RICHARD. So show me your technique.

ROSIE. What?

RICHARD. Your kissing technique.

ROSIE. I knew it! You were spying on me!

RICHARD. *(laughing)* So close your door and don't scream when you're practicing!

ROSIE. *(finally laughing)* Who do you think you are, my big sister?

RICHARD. *(laughing)* You admit it! Finally! You always wanted a big sister!

(as a big sister)

"Now Rosalinda, don't be so bold. Make him come to you. More like this: 'Oh, Kenny.'

(kisses his arm)

ROSIE. *(laughing)* I need a witness!

(stands, calls out window)

Cab! Cab!

RICHARD. *(laughing)* Oh sit down and learn from your big sister!

(pulls her back)

Listen to me and that Kenny-boy won't know what hit him…girlfriend!

ROSIE. *(laughing)* "Girlfriend"? That's it!

(hoists a pillow)

I know what's going to hit you…"girlfriend"!

*(hits **RICHARD** with the pillow)*

RICHARD. Oh: pillow fight? You want to pillow fight…with your big sister?

(hoists another pillow)

If that's what you want…

ROSIE. *(laughing)* No! No!

(mock cowers)

RICHARD. No, no. That's what you want.

(laughing, hits her with the pillow)

Who's the big sister!?

ROSIE. *(cowering, laughing)* You are!

RICHARD. *(laughing)* Who's the big sister?

(hits her with the pillow)

ROSIE. *(laughing)* You are!

*(Giggling and squealing and screaming with laughter, **ROSIE** and **RICHARD** engage in a pillow fight.)*

(fade to black)

The End

ARCANE TRADITIONS

CHARACTERS

WAYNE - High school senior.
CHELSEA - High school senior.

SCENE

High School Gymnasium. Prom Night.
Two chairs to serve as prom thrones.

TIME

The crowning of the king and queen of prom.

COSTUMES

Tuxedo and prom crown for Wayne;
Gown and prom crown for Chelsea.

(SETTING: Prom Night. The throne area of the King and Queen of the prom.)

(AT RISE: WAYNE and CHELSEA, the King and Queen of the prom, sit on their thrones. They wear their crowns, uncomfortably. They've just kissed.)

WAYNE. *(uncomfortable)* Chelsea?

CHELSEA. *(uncomfortable)* Wayne?

WAYNE. I don't know. Would you like some more punch?

CHELSEA. I don't think so. Now now. Maybe later. But, if you'd like some more…

WAYNE. Oh, no. I was just thinking…

CHELSEA. What? Wayne?

WAYNE. I just…I didn't…I didn't want you to think…that wasn't MY idea…

CHELSEA. Oh, The "King and Queen of The Prom Official First Kiss"? It's traditional.

WAYNE. *(scoffing)* Traditional! "King of the Prom."

CHELSEA. *(scoffing)* "Queen of the Prom."

WAYNE. It's all so…

CHELSEA. …superficial.

WAYNE. Yes, that's it! It IS superficial!

CHELSEA. And artificial.

WAYNE. It's very artificial! It's…ancient!

CHELSEA. It's barbaric! Archaic! Arcane!

WAYNE. Arcane?

CHELSEA. *(laughing)* I don't know, either! It was on the SAT!

WAYNE. *(laughing)* Good! For a second there I thought I was kissing Einstein!

CHELSEA. Look, there's Ashley!

(waves to Ashley offstage)

(to WAYNE*)* How long have you two been together?

WAYNE. Since the ninth grade.

(waves)

Hi Ashley!

(to CHELSEA*)* Just like you and Matt.

CHELSEA. *(waves off stage)* Hi Matt!

WAYNE. *(waves)* Hi Matt!

CHELSEA. *(to* WAYNE*)* I guess you and I are just a couple of old love-birds.

(clarifying)

I mean…you and Ashley. And me and Matt. Not really old..

WAYNE. *(finishing her sentence)* …love birds.

(pause)

I know what you mean. You know, it IS kinda funny.

CHELSEA. What?

WAYNE. That the King and Queen of the prom are chosen separately. You know, that they don't have nominations and elections and…

CHELSEA. …and that they don't let COUPLES run! You know, like you and Ashley, me and Matt…

WAYNE. That it isn't just more…logical. Or something. What's a good SAT word for that? "Logical"? Or something?

CHELSEA. *(laughing)* I don't know! Matt's the brain's of the outfit!

WAYNE. *(laughing)* And Ashley's the brainiac of THIS couple! So where does that leave us…?

(nervous pause)

The…gym looks nice tonight. I guess that's one tradition I don't quite hate. I like that we don't rent a ballroom or something downtown.

(looking around)

Some traditions…

CHELSEA. *(shyly)* I was on the Decorating Committee.

WAYNE. *(impressed)* No! Wait, of course you were.

(looking around)

Nice.

CHELSEA. *(shyly)* I chaired Decorations.

(pause)

Matt said it was a waste of my time.

WAYNE. Oh, I disagree.

(looking around)

Impressive. No, I mean it. It's very…artistic.

CHELSEA. I don't know. Matt said…

(pause)

Artistic? Really? Do you really think so?

WAYNE. Well, consider the source: Ashley says I wouldn't know good art from a hole in the ground.

CHELSEA. Well, I disagree.

WAYNE. I really like the way you combine the purple and the sea foam. The symmetries and the asymmetries. Kinda "Art deco versus ghetto chic."

CHELSEA. *(impressed)* "Art deco"?

WAYNE. *(quietly confessing)* No, I've just been taking some art classes downtown, you know…

CHELSEA. Art classes? Downtown? When?

WAYNE. Shh. Every week. Twice a week, I mean. For the last four years.

CHELSEA. *(beaming)* Four years!

WAYNE. *(quietly)* I'm only telling you because I know that you're the big artist in school. Winning all the contests and everything.

CHELSEA. *(shyly)* I'd really like to make it my major in college, but my dad…

WAYNE. Can you keep a secret? I'm going to college on my football scholarship, but once I'm in, I'm going to major in art. Shh.

(pause)

WAYNE. *(cont.)* You should too, Chelsea. You're the REAL artist.

CHELSEA. *(sarcastically)* Right. I don't know. My dad… *(pause)* What about your parents?

WAYNE. *(smiling)* Oh, I just know they'll love the idea.

CHELSEA. Wait! You haven't TOLD them yet!?

WAYNE. You, Chelsea, my Queen of the Prom, are the first to know.

CHELSEA. The first to know? Not even Ashley?

WAYNE. Not even Ashley. It's kind of been my secret. From everybody.

CHELSEA. *(smiling)* For four years?! Pretty good secret, Wayne.

WAYNE. Until now.

(pause)

Everybody has secrets, Chelsea.

(coaxing)

I'm sure you have secrets from Matt.

(falling in love with her)

(music begins)

CHELSEA. That's our cue!

WAYNE. *(more and more in love)* Chelsea? You do have secrets from Matt, right?

CHELSEA. *(taking his hand)* Sh! It's time for The Traditional King and Queen Dance, Wayne! Come on!

(smiling) Come on, "King"!

(gently toying with him) I just know that this is one of those arcane "traditions" you love so much!

WAYNE. *(smiling, knowing he's being toyed with)* Chelsea! Please!

(CHELSEA *takes him by the hand, maneuvers him on to the dance floor.*)

(Tentatively, They take their dance position.)

(They dance.)

WAYNE. *(beaming)* Chelsea.

CHELSEA. *(whispers into his ear, as they dance)* Psst! Wayne?

WAYNE. What?

CHELSEA. *(smiling)* I know what "arcane" means.

WAYNE. *(whispering, smiling)* Me, too.

CHELSEA. *(whispering, smiling)* Secretive.

WAYNE. *(whispering, smiling)* Mysterious. Oooo.

(Smiling, They stop dancing.)

(pause)

(They look into each other's eyes.)

(pause)

(They lean in to kiss.)

(fade to black)

The End

OTHER TITLES AVAILABLE FROM BAKER'S PLAYS

STALKER MOM AND OTHER PLAYS

Diana R. Jenkins

Comedy / Flexible casts of 0-9m, 2-11f / Simple staging

This collection of humorous scripts offers young actors funny characters they'll enjoy playing and contemporary problems they'll find relevant. Clever dialogue, quick pacing, and surprising developments make these scripts fun for performers and audiences alike. The plays utilize flexible casts and simple props, sets, and costumes for easy production.

Sorry! - Jessie struggles to run a club while coping with one member's sorry attitude.

Stalker Mom - Jackson copes with the most over-protective mother on the planet.

Girl in a Whirl - Everyone takes advantage of Abbie, but she's too nice to stand up for herself.

The Grudge - Laird thinks of himself as too easy-going to hold a grudge, but something's growing inside of him!

BAKERSPLAYS.COM

OTHER TITLES AVAILABLE FROM BAKER'S PLAYS

THE RED MERIT BADGE OF COURAGE

Nicolas Hoover

TYA/Children's Theatre, Comedy / 1m, 10f, and 2m or f / Simple Set

The girls of Fireside Scouts Troop #182 are lost. Their day trip to Yellowstone National Park went terribly wrong, and they don't have a scout leader or a map. To make matters worse, they're at the mercy of a careless narrator who didn't go to the bathroom before the play started. How will they survive the rain and the dark? Can they find something to eat before something finds them to eat? Will their story unravel at the hands of a stalling stage manager and two talking trees? After letting off a few ear-splitting screams, these spunky girls gather their wits and their Fireside Scout Handbooks, and prepare themselves to earn the most difficult merit badge of all: The Red Merit Badge of Courage.

www.ingramcontent.com/pod-product-compliance
Lightning Source LLC
Chambersburg PA
CBHW071843290426
44109CB00017B/1907